EXILE

EXILE

Sterling D. Plumpp

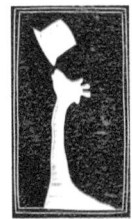

MadHat Press
Cheshire, Massachusetts

MadHat Press
MadHat Incorporated
PO Box 422, Cheshire, MA 01225

Copyright © 2024 Sterling D. Plumpp
All rights reserved

The Library of Congress has assigned
this edition a Control Number of
2024938578

ISBN 978-1-952335-83-9 (paperback)

Words by Sterling D. Plumpp
Cover image: *Fighting Forms* by Franz Marc (1914)
Cover design by Marc Vincenz
Sterling D. Plumpp photograph by James Fraher

www.MadHat-Press.com

First Printing
Printed in the United States of America

*To Duncan and Mali, my grandchildren:
Choose to be anything you want in life.*

To Martin Luther King Jr., whose movement led to the creation of a breathing space for my humanity; to Jamil Abdullah al-Amin (H. Rap Brown); to Hector Pieterson and his Soweto schoolmates, whose deeds and sacrifices should never be forgotten; to Fred L. Banks Jr., whose judicial sobriety always seeks to keep my truths within the legal margins of a court; to Sarah Ann Dickey and Walter Hillman, whose activities created a breathing space for Blacks in my hometown of Clinton, Mississippi; to Jeffery Renard Allen for helping find a publisher for this manuscript; to the publisher of MadHat Press, Marc Vincenz; and to Gwendolyn Mitchell for shepherding me through the process of putting my mouth on paper.

In memory of Leon Forrest, who dared step into the ring with the canonic champions, giving his all, bobbing and weaving his way to literary immortality.

Table of Contents

Foreword by Mongane Serote — xi

1. I anoint my spirit — 3
2. Thirteen years ago — 4
3. I was born a lingerer — 6
4. He was blind — 11
5. There are many Mississippis — 13
6. They wanna always — 19
7. There are no dead — 23
8. I am always beginning — 25
9. In twenty-two days — 28
10. Every day — 30
11. My name is all — 36
12. We are here — 39
13. Blues is a critical — 41
14. My journey — 44
15. I grow to maturity — 46
16. Forty-three years ago — 50
17. They took my mother — 55
18. This odyssey — 58
19. Buried in the ninety — 61
20. Half a decade — 62
21. The Little Rock — 64
22. Every day / they house — 65
23. Every / thing is here — 67
24. Every poem is — 68
25. There is no permanence — 71
26. I journey — 73

Afterword by Michael Anania — 77
About the Author — 79

Foreword

Sterling, I read *Exile* ... here then I say...

To leave against your will. To stay wherever by whoever's command and stay against your will. To have had your tongue, your eyes, and ears all, even your soul, almost wiped empty and then made to keep standing whether you will or not ...

And then, one day on our own, on your own, you keep standing ... wherever it is you suddenly find yourself and then you choose to live ...

After a most painful deep breathing and exhaling, hanging on living and life then you walk because you took a decision, I will keep standing ... and I will keep walking, tongue or no tongue, eye or no eye, ear or no ear ... by my soul and will I stand and walk and live ... and find my mind and soul ...

I, I determine that..., I, I am my people even as I am alone like this, I am them and am many ...

Ah, Sterling, my brother

You gave us all our voice

Soul and sound

Sight and thought

Mongane Serote
Poet, writer, National Poet Laureate of South Africa

All I got
is a fragment
of a bit
ten miles

of a hole I
revive
with dreams to
gather
a vision

Exile

1.

I anoint my spirit
        to fill dreams
        at foreign service
        stations of the cross
 roads

I put on the goodfoot
        prints of an odyssey
        across land across
              water across time
        and distance to arrive

This magnolia memory
        is my DNA blossoming
              in music.

2.

Thirteen years ago
        this eloquent man
    din
go speech of guitar and drum
            beats
        withdrew from audible circles

Exile is home
        to diasporic voices
strangeness makes decipherable
        hummed fluidity
trekking sheets of diurnal riffs
riffs riffed over and over
        void of longings
and identity knitted
kente memory piecing to
        gather ancestry
tattered presence of days
        and nights commence
this lost spirit's conversation
    as sermon

Rhapsodic emission out of
        kitchenette skies
        expanding high
ways of yes Lord   it is a
    sermon
calling
calling
calling

All to gather a kente weaving
        of memoir

Thirteen long years
a twelve-bar oracle
        carrying crosses over and
        and over each day

Strangeness here
strangeness there
strangeness every where

Twelve-bar muse go missing
thirteen years ago

while I riff in wind
        and I catch
a basket full of words
        in the net

work of my prayers
        and I run to the market
places in dreams and I hum
        to tell black berries
to Christian black sell my bucket
for my soul been anchored
        in the lore
my soul been anchored

3.

I was born a lingerer
        for the call with
in callings   crops of utterances
        trampled by dust
I invent heavenly
        in silences
        and ambulate
my times in dreams
        for I know
places I should meet
        on this odyssey
impelled on wind
and riffed solos of infinity
        I collect

I believe in the sacred
        oracle: the black
smith's prophecy
        jumping out of
his chromatic anvil

Wailing footsteps pounding
        and hammering
way ancestors imposed
hymns of weaving
        on distance and
long sea
faring journeys from
        lost tongues of self
casting net of tears

                to catch
echoes of chanting drums
                fare ye
wailing islands of ritual
                and rites

and I imbibe
            dietary excerpts
       from epic genes
            of becoming

I am an old man
            and the see
see rider absent.
            Mirrors impotent
to revive youth

I live a current
emitting mud
from Memphis to
        New
Orleans open mouth
        piece
I beg to embouchure
        my pen
        this hour
        my crescent
lyrics come out

adorned in brass
        knuckles I borrow
        to slay executioners of my name
                and time and place

I am an old man
        and the see
    my fingers squeeze
        from latent
narratives rising in my vision

My daddy's daddy
        was hung on a cross
            cut saw and my
momma's momma
        was boptized in
            in hums
her do Lord, do Lord
        do remember mes
           knitted quilts of language
          even in stormy weather

    Prayer time
    only place call
existence from strong arm
        strong   nobody
know the trouble
    I see
and glimpse of a
        single tree

hitches my melancholy
to barges
tugging idioms of
speech to stations
      of lyricism

my daddy's daddy
mimes his cross
      cut saw's
melodic oration and

my momma's momma
in tears of an apron
      dripping
from the holy holy hand
      me down
beliefs in sacred
      looking glasses
that reflect dance

Every time I cry
   Lord, Lord have mercy
   I sho aint callin
      the Lord
   though I know
bended knees
arms of heaven's
        blessing
    I possess them
I sing and sing

I woke up this morning
I woke up this morning
I woke up this morning

there is another world
         to explore
to live

The aegis of a dream
         anoints me
         to cross over
the one more mile
         to cross and
discover and name
         still waters
survey and name
         them as a
men's occupation
         as highways
to things of night and
         and wind
         and distance
                 my pen pledges
allegiance to

I am a poet
a dream guarantor
         of vision

4.

He was blind
        all
            ways in blues
clubs some
        time wearing
one shoe and bare
footed on the other
        one

They say
        sold dictionaries
and encyclopedias
        he carried
            in soles
of his shoes

They say
        his principle
            items silence and
nothing and he
        could see
out of   eyes in foot
        prints and track
of his tears

I take the red eye
        glass of muscadine
wine to journey
find the blues
        a midnight service

```
          station of the cross
                  roads
to refill myths
        in spirits
so they breathe
        in time
```

5.

There are many Mississippis
        I left
regurgitated on levees
        of pain
and its tributaries
        of dialects
I speak

I belong to the ode
        in the wind
I sing the blues
        this journey
        this odyssey
aspires to infinitely
        no boundaries
no chains linked
to impositions

When my pen digs
        into rich
soiled furrows of
        miles
        it captures
the future mood

erecting mountains of
possibility I throw
        to airmail
        bags of electrified
            smoke

                stack light my
                to jolt my memory

melody my grand
            mother's needle
                imposes on diasporic
                        cloth scraps
                    called the kente patterns
                        in her mother
witted lodes
        of imagination
there are many chasms
on my globe
I can never cartograph
                    them
Negro spirituals
            visionary   arias of
tomorrow call my name
            in narrative I remember
            I got tattered
 blues ascensions
            from doubt

this gospel Trane
        get on birds
whispering Satchmo's
nuances to self

            I solo so long
                I solicit

                tones of his indigo
                        down Moses
                icon riffs
I am father
                        and descendants
                        of narratives
I meditate
        to tell more
I am a poet
on this epic odyssey
                this magic distance
breathing identity
                from over
Lords of winds and miles
                and miles

Spring's tears
        are abundant here.

I access rich delta water
melons of the blues
                sweet meanings
                a memory to persevere

For I am the soil
        and weather
veins that counsel
                every flood
                drop to bring
                        life

I claim disparate
        geographies
and own no totems
        of ancestry
for diasporic dreams
        and hopes
have no wardrobe of lineage
to define limits
        on creativity

Each has a new beginning
        for my pen
to embalm in memory

        To explore
        my names and remember what
            ever ink
                desires to spill
                      on pavement
            of silence I travel
        through time and distance

        the surely I am
            has no moment

I live in labyrinths
        layered with
in labyrinths

      I come   come and
      I sing history of
           my odyssey

      I am diasporic
           African
      in dream and myth struggling
           gestate
Blues, part of
      the narrative
      architectured self
           were foot
      noted in manuals of
           strangeness

Every day I try to hail
           and whole on
      shouting here to
      gather in holy
           rolled pews
           pulpited
to flower
I accept with humility
      my need
to sometimes cry

      I sing blues
           on porches of invention
                  I sing

I am a poet

Blues is sorghum
        made nightly
                in the mind
      as well as
      back alley out
      lines of a glass of gin

6.

They wanna always
  wanna the slaver
  wanna take in
    side you
your epic
nodding and cycles
  of talking

take your wondering memory
   survey where you
been cartographing
lyricism and dreams

where you been a
   round globe
wanna take your lies
   say
    I sing the blues

I/keep them whole
in paths of my narrative
my lineage
is an eternal migrant
in search of possibilities

   I am a poet

My narrative
  telling and
  telling

to become growth
instances of imagination

freedom and democracy
        don't live here any
                more

As the poets say
        the word is here
poem got foot
        prints in myth
I am always reaching
        I am an artist
I make days
        light from miles

I am a poet

Skin breaks
breathing ceases
        is rhythmic
        melody
get odes of dreams
        congregate
        and march on

This is the odyssey
        I am

I am
        all the narrative
        gone and all
                to come

I am a poet

I got a contract
        with distance
        with time
        with scattered bits
                of ancestral identity

I word myself a
        way
I sing
every line is
        an epic
a million pages
        of aborted narratives

There are no margins
        in infinity
        yet I breathe
lyric precise search
        lights of vision
this is the beauty
        of self
this is the beauty
        of identity

You
        earn it well dark
        telling and
        telling and
        telling
Blues   muddy
        oration
all my life
I been secreting
        this song
this song
where I build roads of odes
        here I been working
        on the building

7.

    There are no dead
             ends
there no tomorrows
       in the nocturnal
street I peruse

Fifty-one year ago
      I married
left loneliness for a spell
       but still waters
hound my dreams
       let me know
I was on the porteous road
       the endless odyssey
      cycled and
recycled in twelve bar
       revelations
I am
      condemned
to be dragged through
wind and nights and
       miles and miles

Literacy bestows me
        a vehicle
I am no longer
        hitched
to impromptu whims
        or immobile ideas
on a syllabus of dictates

        I can fly

8.

I am always beginning
I rewind gestures
        of self in mind
                and body and
soul Coleman
riffs into a
        mystic
lyricism

this hope I refined
        when I
take doses of creativity

Sixty-five years ago
        the grunts and moans
        and short breath
rituals of inhalation
        left me
forever alone

Poppa had given seven
        decades plus four
years to land
        tenancy codes
of survival
        his pray a cell
phone call
        to his God
emitting ladders
        from skins imprisonment
he internalizes decades of
        the king
highway's lore

was a practitioner of
        the word

closed his eyes
        as believer

the frigid wind
        of his burial
affirms society's willingness
        to hammer
his presence into
        insignificance

Memory of him
        is a vast geography.

this distance
this continuing odyssey
        from his passing
        is my identity

9.

In twenty-two days
        I enter
my eighth decades
wandering in this skin
wondering how long
        until this odyssey
cycle and cycle

I am this canvass
        partial make
        a way some
hows I rescue
from depths
Where I couldn't
        hear nobody pray
I went into moments
        I dream
I store my longing
        in a vase
tell my poem
        I gotta make
bouquets outta
        bruised flowers
of hope
it say
you get miles
        and miles and
        miles down wrinkled

maps you dream
you got miles
    and miles and
    miles in open windows
   of the wind

10.

Every day
        one epic
an accomplice
its stanzas small
        talk herd through the great
vein canals of gossip
        whispered so as
to glimpse twelve
bar silhouettes
        of language

Every day
        I dream pages
        of history
and laughter touring
        ruins for
        a blues star
                I own

Sometimes
sometimes I feel
another epic passing by
        I flag a stage
where I greet Macbeth

Been down so long
        darkness opens
        a day and miles
give me papers
        to enter
    boundaries of identity

I am a poet
an employee of myth
        I sing
I sometimes feel
        I am a prophet
because I travel
        this journey
where all narratives
        are true
(as Achebe and Wideman reveal)
and I didn't know
if I am only
on furloughs from lost
        rites
and furloughs can be
days or months
        or decades or centuries
I travel sovereign
        in my belief
committed to distance

I exist
        I come here

        I come to hear
for sojourn
        over infinite miles
and evidential
        lyrics
silence dare not
        approach

My generation
        is passing
near the engine of
today's awakening
hear my pen calling
over near the cross
        ties
where there are no
        Tranes coming

You are a poet
        when your speech
leads choirs from silence
        over distance in
                to miles and miles
You are a poet
 when the page
        dissolves formality

My poems are dew
        drop inns
in territory of tragedy

I am
        tattered vestment
longing a ward
        robe
and my illusion
profiles a geography
        of my personal globe

I am a poet
when my pen furrows
        blues
noted dramas
        the future's
air mail
to a band of gypsies
Jimi collages
        with smoked
vision of genius
a blind heart
can grasp
        in thunderstorms

This journey alone
        is communal
I fine my shadow some
        where
                in some
body's weighed bout
of misery

tiers
of the odyssey
        I meet to compose
narratives to be
        mirrored waste
lands of the hour

Ore clad apertures
        of hope
I long to hand
my dreams

I am a sequence
        to an end
filed in personal catalog
        of imagination

I use to rite
        what is
reed with my pen

I am here
       after hours
       when tenor screams
to rafter round midnight
       a Monk's chortle
genius invokes misterioso
       collages
of Be Bopping surges
       to place his marqueed
icon of sound on the air
       so I can
genuflect

11.

My name is all
        the faces
in diasporic
mirrors
erected in lore
        kente
woven in spirit

I am this attitude
for I name my ills
        in exile
I enumerate bits
        of my soul
and pieces scattered
and incensed with memoirs
        of twenty-three
thousand distinct linguistic
        statues of ancestry
        in silence
and I rise urban
        until my pen
        fills a concrete minute
        roots in a delta memory

for my mythology and my kin
        were vast
into non distinct
        existence
I conjure to a callaloo
        delicacy

some
  where a pulse clogs
    in veins
I am the scream
  closeted in sound
of this pain

I locate reigns
  of lyric vision
soaked in Booker T's
  green onion
blues narrative
  more onion
in their forked
  origin

Every day I rise
  from a discography
tugging an epic
  tragedy with
  in gains of laughter

I am a poet
I mix ingredients
of pain and nuance
into the pot
  holes up on the
  root

I call narrative
    to opening in my
    odyssey
I feast on lean time
    out of a black yard
    blue note

Odes etched here
    by alien nations
from hours and
    longings
    I steal from the melody

I am the song
    I long   the epic
    I allude to
in metamorphosis
    of riffs
I pursue up to
    seven steps to heaven

12.

We are here
we breathe here
    after hours
we breathe brown
    cistern watered
vocabularies of telegrams
    to foster
the uncertainty
    we are

I never accept
    the colored
body with no identity
for my poems

Nine below zero
    and I catch a cold
    Trane ascending to upper
    rooms of the
    upper
suite Mahalia pleads
    for precious hallelujahs
    all over
this land of mines
    to designate
tomorrows all over
    this land of mines

Maybe my pen
 got an inspiration
 to rise in sorrows again

No matter how many
 miles traveled
the road to beauty
 is a share
  cut a
  cross of tears and
dust tracks
 of the roads
 I must genius travel

13.

Blues is a critical
        mood
and unfinished
        opening
        in the wreck
ages of selves

The odyssey I find
        the narrative
my voice
my myth
my power

When I am thirsty
        I prefer a Bud
Be Bop dipper chord
        with max beats
of conversation to some
        where / some
        where

We are doomed
        to negotiate roads
without maps
        though we chart
        trajectory
of our odyssey
        in lost words

We long cartographed
＄＄＄＄hints lodged
＄＄＄in skeletons

We imagine futures.

＄＄＄＄We embark
＄＄＄＄＄on dreams and
＄＄＄＄＄they became bibles

How
many prophecies
＄＄＄＄been lost
this is no linear
＄＄＄＄narrator
＄＄＄＄in my narrative

though when a
＄＄＄＄woke to articulation
＄＄＄＄my pen is investments
＄＄＄＄in a foreign tongue

Trying to window
＄＄＄a world
＄＄＄is my word
that slopes this cross
＄＄＄＄roads of prophecy
＄＄＄＄and lowdown feeling

America is a pastured
      fragment
   a pause
   in my odyssey

I am
the ultimate voice

      societies exist
      to perpetuate
      their narrative

I exist
    to discover
    mine
beneath beats of
    tradition
in creole dialect
    myth making
    trials
my pen wrestles

14.

My journey
    is a summit
        between dreams and memory
           where I negotiate
        specifics episodes

I repeat
distance and
miles and miles

I row my name
        through blues of
        new beginnings
Nearly fifty-five
    years ago
    at the holy Pettus
        bridge a major
    oath for future
    generations recited

    (I believe a
    spirit carries your voice still)
For this road
    I travel
    is eternity

Every morning
		when I rise
	from mists

I make an apron and
hymn it with stitches of
babeled threads of
		language I collect
for the montage of
		narratives
		I drink
		are my day
			light

When you orbit morality
		you orbit some
wide elliptical maneuvers
		to morality

15.

I grow to maturity
        in jack
son breeders
        of myth
        that old time tid
                bit of diasporic
cleansing tones
        emitted Saturday nights
or Sunday morning glory
blossoming efficacy
of their scattered search
        for longing
clothes of speech

and
decisions at dawns
        of despair
pealing from recalcitrant pews
many miles to growth
        in fertilized
eyes of ritualize
        cross
cut melodies of healing

in depths
       of Fat Albert
King's solos a
       cross eternal
       existence

Music is forever
       and forever

They severed my legs
       left me a stub
       born of memory
            sometimes in darkness
I meet strangers
don't know if
       they be evil
       switch
blade in diasporic
       hours and thereby
mumble
       peg an existence
 from doubt

time shows us
       this road
this ascent of creativity

this odyssey here
        in millions of robes
        on windows of
        imagination and
            myth
where the blues
    is a hand
imprisoned in the corner
    stone of roads
silhouetted fingers
    of ancestry

I feel my existence
I feel my journey
whatever America
    was to be
it had no name
    until I go there
with layering
    out the impossibility
daily burdens

When decades pass
    I wave good
    byes and sanction
spontaneity of my journey
    alone
    on this odyssey
where I long and pray

She aint said nothing
        yet just
stands with her history
        incarnate in a glass of
episodes of pain
        she boldly toasts
as she
penetrates from close
aisles of yesterday
her expression
        an opening
final troubles packed
        in pauses of her
        stare
suggests possibility of
        liberation by lips
tones escape some
        long wang
dang doodle flower
        of skin

can ruin in a surface
        wind
she is the cycle
        on endurance and
        deliverance

16.

Forty-three years ago
    I woke
to the toi toi head
    lines
depicting landscapes
    of rage and
defiance

Soweto gave me
    good news
clocked in blood

There are so many
    chasms in my existence
I cannot cartograph them
    Negro spirituals
these visionary noises
call my name

in stains I rise
    from pain
blues arias
    lift my vision
so I can covet healing

Howlin Wolf
    his smoke stack
lightning globes
    of innovation
grant me a ticket

        to self
to selves I own
then same gospel Trane
        hovering over
his flue of his
        lyric fire
ornament tones
allow me
        to solicit
        rare indigo
        down
Moses lyrics

So
there is not necessity
        for me to take
my mother
wit on this odyssey
        without a library

sometimes prayer
        is a thimble
I use
to stitch hours
of matrix eyes
as logos on the sky
        after dusk

all my journey
        a road

                a road
        my dream must take

I take this cross
        down below moan
        use it as a vessel
the ties I wear
        for my journey's end
when my pen
        digs into
the inked road
        it captures
the future's air
        mail band
of gypsies

Jimi calligraphies
        with voyages
                I shout

In the narrative
        you can
not be sure of
anything except
callings of language
        you pursue
over miles and miles

The quest is
        an insurance
        policy

This country loves me
        so it legislates
            my surname
as anonymity

This incredible sojourn
        this incipient music
I pilfer from the dread
        locked doors of Jah

This I accept and
        solicit all
        ways

This odyssey
this story
this quest for closure
this diurnal prevalent of
        the spirit
I seek to bandage
        my pen is comforter
to wounds
        in this myth's rare
            tier
        drops I negotiate

                for a glass
to drink aboriginal
        queries from
     chaos

In her hair
        was ribboned
                caine mutiny
            of knots
the essence of my
        pen's quest

17.

They took my mother
        wit
they took my mother
        tongue
there are no lungs
        for my voice

there is no place
        time has no
        residence here

I never dream

I swing
        into margins of pass
            word
        that is my cry

I, twelve bar
        custodian of bad
        news and trouble
        poke openings in blocked
            venues of vision

That old rugged
        cross
        road
sacred object of ancestral
            memory
        image of myth

                    making unadorned

Mississippi is a tangled
            metaphor
you dig to rescue
            miles of a budding
flowers ascending from sand
            stone feelings if a
                        place
you know
and don't know
this is home
            bass for me

This is where I left
            my names
this is where my dreams
            return

Mississippi is home with
            out a homeland
security blanket
of justice

I can never pen
            down
thing for sure
            I pivot a
round in this odyssey

I catch a melody
        in windows
and wind and sing
orchestrated fire side
        chats with riffs
        I imagine

This my task
        master   this never
ending quest
        to begin again

I board
        miles and miles
                contract distance
        for signs
        to vision

I go a
        long song
the wind and
distance and
depth and
width of a language
        I dream
        to exist

18.

This odyssey
this story
        folded in desire

so I Louie, Louie
        Jordan   so I can
                cross to hear

Caldonia's
        hard head
lines in the ball
        paint's applauses
Caldonia, Caldonia
        what makes your
        big head
so hard

I long and
I love the story
        I am

the poem is epidermis
        of possibility

I sketch its continuing
        narrative
manifolded in infinite
        obituaries

to reach
this road
this poem

this story
        is true

I am
its echo and
its reflection
its metaphor

I guide quest
        scout caverns
        in line
breaks and myth
        wearing
canvass of verbs

I am
the dream and
scope of its smoke

I am an ode
of oath and miles
        and miles and
        miles

This memory is
the decade I
      left
the future
      I long
maneuvers in chromatic
      lines
mapped veins
of the word
      I caress

I build sentences
      of improvised
reigns dropped
into my hands

I come blue
I come black

19.

Buried in the ninety
        nine tons of
burden my soul
       hauls
          over the rain
              bow
          ties of need

passages of wars
passages of pain
passages of hunger
passages of rites

my address is
           metamorphosis

I rise
I fall
I row
I cycle boundaries

20.

Half a decade
      after I
contemplate you
lowered six feet

I am near a precipice
      of will
through a two decade
      diplomacy
with a plateau

Momma say
      he left you
      a present all
            ways wanted
            your survival
wanted you
    hear melody
of lark or sparrow

When you put
that paper in my hand
      I gave
      it to you

I am elated
        neatly wrapped
an empty paper
        bag
then it belong to me
and I am with
out a wood
clearing of language

Momma say
        he know
you get mad
cuss him
but that all
        he own

She say
        nothing is beginning
        nothing is the end

You can put
        tablets of dream
          there in between and
              they grow
say he say
times he thought
        nothing in my head

21.

The Little Rock
        nine congregate
in her heart

embark to central high
each day from there

LC's lean buck
        shot assurance
resided at the front
        window

Central high is
a gamble
the nine deal or
roll lasting
        avowals
            to prevail

22.

Every day
they house
        files of threads
        abuse in silences

dumps them
in her ears
the uncharted path
to victory faces
curses and insinuations
        of death

This saga
this story of long
distance strides

she knows
        from deep rivers
crossed before

She hides
   in her mothering them

times threats trail
        her car
curses and plain
        gestures to rip
her from it abound

Ms. Toni pear
handle sets beside her
and she dials a prayer line
      regiments of angel
          winged
for mason of justice
      who accompany
her to
another day

23.

Every
thing is here
even
prodigal
scripture of line
        age reside in here
say hey   hey
      the blues is all
              right

24.

Every poem is
        a fus
    elage of dreams
          I pilot
over in oasis of
         moment
I pen down
        with a
        mood

hours decorated
         with sweat
this august dog
         on membrane of
ancient selves
drifting into field
         hollers
where tomorrows on
         hoisted
on shoulders of
         viral amens

a single tree
        might hold
up tornadoes
        for a ticket
to ride whole
        wheat chats

and
where momma
is calico
chairman of the
needle of prayers

at the end of small
        hours blues is
        an eloquent
romance with tragedy

and my foot
        notes of pain
        wear
golden slippers

Every time I
        pick up my pen
I delegate
to a piece summit

and I wonder
if there are deities
without myth

I collate bits
        to fuel
        my odyssey

I wander
in identity
        scattered
a diasporic distance

this journey
        is madness

I am a poet
        imprismed
in geographic address
        changes

25.

There is no permanence
      in treks
        from slave
ships through Mississippi
      delta saturated
continuances and creolized
in invention of lore

To southside spaces
of twelve for idioms
      churned Saturday
nights or Sunday
morning glories
      ascending poles
      of hours and miles

The beauty of poetry
      is its uncertainty

The poet voyages and
      voyages

I never tire
I reach past
metaphors for sound
        and syntax not
        yet born

Maybe I dreams
        gourds of language
        I drink
till words garland
        wreathes
initiated on mirror
        of my desire

my longing to tell

I breathe stanzas
        dance line
break configuration

the poem
        is the poet's DNA

we were here
        to tell

26.

I journey
I conjure
I call
I hasten

I know I don't
        know
I reach

my words
are carving
on momma's apron
        strings
a palimpsest
        resurrection of hushes
                and prayers

The subtle laughter
        of her silence
          a blue
print for my quest
to journey

There. In your eyes
the story of
your day told

toi toi steps
        of Soweto
to scatter all
over power of gun
shots and town
ships to edict
        civic lessons of
will on pages of
blood drenched
earth

tolled death
kneel gasps
of apartheid

There. Shadows
        pata pata
round midnight
lanterns in aisles

of the young
who are young
        no more

There.   The tough
tale of your hours
is an epic danced
in expanding
margins of dreams

you plant
        in MEDU delta
rich pores of a
peoples
in birth postures of
a new nation

There. The sound of
torrid insistence
        rains.

Slow blues wear
        a risk
watch to tale
every body how
little pains clog
        their hours

their wounded
occupation
of beginning.

Afterword

In 1982, with *The Mojo Hands Call, I Must Go,* Sterling Plumpp began a poetic engagement with the blues and jazz, a calling, at once literary and spiritual, carried through a series of remarkable books, including *Ornate With Smoke* and *Horn Man.* The effort has been to find an identity between poem and music, not merely as subject but as a guide into both lament and swirling bebop improvisation. *Exile* is a late stage in that journey, a book-length, solo riff on the self, found and isolated within music and Black history and heritage. Here, the pen, now as fully musical as the horn, has in speech the mouth's embouchure, though it is still, recalling the rural South, a plow, a rough stylus writing in furrows. Language, as it draws on the shreds and tatters of tradition, is both made of "pain and nuance" and "mystic lyricism." In one of the great Plumpp emjambments, "I word myself a / way," a dissolution and a path. This is an astonishing book, quick, vivid, and nuanced, the poet, like the jazz artist, declaring his space with sustained, restless invention.

Michael Anania
Poet, essayist, and fiction writer

About the Author

STERLING D. PLUMPP—blues poet and essayist—is the author of fourteen books including *Home/Bass, Velvet Bebop Kente Cloth, Ornate with Smoke* and *Blues Narratives*. He is the editor of two anthologies, *Somehow We Survive*, a collection of South African writing and *Steel Pudding: Writing from the Gary Historical and Cultural Society Writer's Workshop*. Plumpp is Professor Emeritus at the University of Illinois at Chicago, where he served on the faculty in the African American Studies and English Departments. He served as a visiting professor in the Master of Fine Arts Program at Chicago State University, and he served as the Writer-in-Resident at Mississippi Valley State University.

In 2009, *Valley Voices* produced an entire issue of its journal, The Sterling Plumpp Issue, focused on his poetry, interviews and critical explorations of his work. In 2016, the University Press of Mississippi published *Conversations with Sterling Plumpp*, edited by John Zheng. Plumpp is the recipient of numerous awards as a blues poet and African American cultural storyteller including The Before Columbus Foundation's 2014 American Book Award for Literature. In October 2018, he was inducted into the Chicago Blues Hall of Fame and recognized for his work as a Blues Scholar. In 2022, Plumpp was honored by his hometown of Clinton, Mississippi, with his inclusion on the Clinton Blues Legacy Marker, which is part of the historic Mississippi Blues Trail. In April 2025, Plumpp will be honored for his contributions to Black culture and to American Arts & Letters and has been invited to be the featured poet in the Cave Canem Legacy Series.

www.ingramcontent.com/pod-product-compliance
Lightning Source LLC
Chambersburg PA
CBHW020338170426
43200CB00006B/427